THE
SIX
SISTERS
CLORA
MILLER

THE SIX SISTERS
Copyright © 2022 **Clora Miller**

ISBN (Paperback): 978-1-958082-16-4
ISBN (Ebook): 978-1-958082-17-1

Printed in the United States of America

CONTENTS

THE
SIX
SISTERS
CLORA
MILLER
THE
SIX
SISTERS
CLORA
MILLER
THE
SIX
SISTERS
CLORA
MILLER
THE
SIX
SISTERS
CLORA

Chapter 1

IT ALL STARTED with Jesse and Helen falling in love. Jesse, born March 19, 1919, in Opelousas, Louisiana, was an uneducated man with a big heart. He came home to Helen after serving in World War II. Helen was also born in Opelousas, Louisiana on September 13, 1926, to a very prominent family. She was a beautiful creole lady and well educated. Jesse was from the other side of the tracks and not a suitable mate for Helen. Her parents were well educated with a different lifestyle. Once married, Jesse moved his wife to Texas. Of course, Helen's family was upset and disapproved. Little did she know her goals of teaching school and writing poetry were over.

After the first year of marriage, Jesse told Helen it was time to have children. Along came their first daughter, Jesse Lyn. A pretty baby girl with hazel eyes. Times were difficult for Jesse and his wife in the year 1948. He found a job, construction work, with six months left to complete the layout. Jesse did not want his wife to work.

Three years later, another girl named Diana was born. She was very beautiful, with naturally curled black hair. Jesse was a proud father.

A year later, Brenda was born. She was the ugly duckling that turned into a swan later in life with a lot of hard work. Jesse was laid off from work and kept moving the family from place to place to look for jobs. Finally, in the year 1953, Shelia was born. Shelia was born with Bette Davis' eyes. During this period, Jesse moved his family to a house in Houston, Texas. With four girls, Helen was tired and somewhat disappointed with her life. She was struggling to provide for her daughters.

But it was not over. In 1955, Clora was born. Helen and Jesse were very pleased with the beautiful baby girl with green eyes. Then, Renita, the sixth girl, was adorable when she was born a year later. Helen was left by herself to take care of six little girls.

Jesse, who was feeling tired, decided to look for a job out of town. Helen was the youngest of ten children in her family. She grew up with five sisters and four brothers.

Her mother came to Houston to help with the six girls. Times were tough, but the girls always had clean clothes and food on the table. They were happy girls running and playing games with each other.

In 1960, Jesse was out of work and the family had to move to another house with the help of Helen's mother. For the first time, Jesse was a homeowner. Things were back on track, and Helen appreciated the help from her mother.

Jesse worked in construction while the daughters were in school. Helen was in charge of the kitchen and the housekeeping. Helen didn't have a life outside of her family. Whenever a problem involving the daughters arose while Jesse was out of town, Helen would read her bible and pray the rosary. Every Saturday and Sunday, the girls went to a Catholic church.

By the time Renita was ten years old, Jesse hurt his back. He dislocated a disk in his back lifting a heavy pipe. After surgery, he filed for disability. Helen is a good mother but sadly most of the time. Jesse loves his family and wanted to make more money. A pool hall business was his choice. Things were never the same. Helen's opinion did not matter. Jesse made all the decisions. The two eldest girls became a problem, and Jesse was gambling with the fellows.

Helen was stressed and did not know what to do. Her only joy was Clora; the fifth daughter was always telling jokes and never saw the real picture. Eventually, Jesse has an affair and spends less time with his family. His drinking was out of control, and Helen was dealing with Jesse's issues, the girls, housework, and cooking. Yes, it got worst for the family. The family went to Louisiana for their grandmother's funeral. Helen felt the weight on her shoulders. The girls lost the only grandmother they spent time with. They were young when Jesse's mother passed. They heard the stories.

3

All this took place during the summertime, so the girls were back to their daily routine within a week. When all of the six sisters were young, everything felt normal, like a traditional family.

Even though their father was not around very much, Helen enjoyed playing games with her daughters and watching them grow up. Each child had a different personality and point of view. What happened to the laughter? The dreams never came true.

By the time Jesse Lyn, the oldest daughter, reached seventeen, she was having sex and dropped out of school. She eventually got married and left home.

Diana was only fifteen with many problems. As a little girl, she wanted attention all the time from her father. She was using heavy drugs, having sex with different boys, missing days from school, stealing, fighting, and had no respect for her parents or sisters.

Brenda was fourteen in high school running track to escape problems in her life and the chaos. Every day trying different product to make her hair grow. The sisters would tease Brenda and call her ugly names. Her father contributed to the ridicule. He made fun of her speech. Clora felt sorry for Brenda. Clora was the only sister she felt close to.

Shelia was thirteen years old and a simple child. She was embarrassed by her skinny legs and big knees. Shelia would like more attention from her parents.

Clora was twelve years of age. She liked to play with dolls. Her father used to go to the Camp Fire Girls banquets with Clora.

Helen was very proud of Clora. She participated in school plays, was an honor student, an obedient child, and always kept a smile on her face. We called the baby girl *"Peanut"* because she was little and sucked her thumb all the time.

At the early age of eleven, Renita fantasized she was the only child. Maybe one sister named Clora. Jesse adored his wife and daughters whenever he was home. Helen worshipped the ground that man walked on. It was kind of sad.

As time went on, things got out of control. Helen and her daughters were the talks of the neighborhood. A year later, Jesse Lynn left her husband and came back home with a drug habit. Diana was pregnant with an older man, high on drugs, and carrying an unborn child. The other four girls were fine for the time being. Helen was at a loss for what to do. Their father came home and took charge of the situation with Jesse Lyn and Diana.

Meanwhile, the four sisters could hear the arguing and fussing. Helen, being a Catholic, did not believe in abortions, so Diana had the baby. Jesse Lyn left home again and became a stripper. Both girls were still using drugs. Everybody loved Diana's baby, except her mother. There, Helen was raising another girl all over again. Diana was an outlaw, always in trouble, and a total embarrassment to herself and the family. The police had the family's address and name on file. The only time Helen had peace of mind was when Diana was incarcerated.

Brenda was working part-time at the neighborhood grocery store. Her hair grew long. Running track had Brenda physically in shape, and she blossomed. After graduation, Brenda got married, anxious to leave home.

Shelia felt poor and raggedy with busted shoes since she could no longer wear Brenda's clothes to school. Shelia had her issues to deal with and prefer to be left alone. She was a stubborn child and talked back to her mother, which was not wise. No one could sass Hellen and win. Shelia would make matters worse. Shelia was teased a lot by her sister Diana. Her father called her Bill English. He said the way Shelia walked reminded him of the cold man with two left feet. She liked when her daddy called her Lighting because she thought it meant running faster than her sisters. Her sisters knew Shelia was not steady on her feet, rather clumsy. After graduation, she immediately married Melvin before he left for the army. Shelia went to the hive with her husband's sister. That was the last time Shelia wore a dress. She never let her legs be exposed. Helen became more relaxed, giving Renita and Clora birthday parties. Jesse could afford Christmas presents because there were times when Christmas was late. Clora was always happy for her dolls.

Chapter 2

TIME WAS PASSING BY. In 1971, the two youngest sisters were busy with school. Things at home seem to be OK for Renita and Clora. The boys were checking the girls out. At the age of fifteen, Clora met her first boyfriend named Mark. She was very close to her mother. Helen could always look Clora in the face and know when something was on her daughter's mind. They talked about this boy for a while.

Mark came to visit Clora on a Sunday after church. Shelia and Renita sat in the living room watching Mark and Clora. Mark felt uncomfortable with Helen staring at him. He asked Clora if she could go out for ice cream. Mark, Clora, and her sisters rode to the ice cream parlor. They were excited her boyfriend had a car and working on a job.

The next Saturday, the girls went to the movies. The three sisters had girl talk after Mark left. Every Sunday, the family got together and gave an update on their children and events over dinner. Helen enjoyed cooking for the family. When Clora became sixteen, marriage was on her mind. She hoped Helen would understand. Mark proposed and she felt ready. The question Helen asks her daughter was, *"are you pregnant?"* Clora just looked at her mother and smiled. Mark was pressing her for sex. That secret Clora knew to keep to herself.

She confessed, *"I am saving myself for my wedding."* Helen had plans for Clora to go to college; she had the academic grades. Helen wanted a better life for her daughter. Her mother tried her best to talk Clora out of the marriage and go to college. Reluctantly, Helen gave her approval and signed for the marriage license. That was in 1972. Her mother insisted they live at home the first year and save money. This plan would please Helen.

Clora attended a vocational school and received her GED one year earlier, along with her certificate for a nurse aide.

In 1973, Clora and Mark moved to their apartment not far from her parents.

Clora did not have a driver's license. Her parents brought a car. Jesse taught Clora how to drive at the age of fifteen because he was gone most of the time.

Helen did not drive. He knew she felt comfortable riding in the car din with Clora.

Right now, there were a lot of problems with the family.

Renita dropped out of middle school and was heavy on drugs. Diana was out of prison and Renita was pregnant. Shelia was getting checks from her husband, and Renita had a social security check. The sisters shared an apartment. Jesse was working on her third husband and was on drugs. Brenda was pregnant and living across town.

On Sunday, all of the sisters would have dinner as planned. Helen was nervous. Diana called to talk about taking her daughter to live with her. Helen turned the ringer on the telephone off. Their father doesn't like it when his daughters drank alcohol. Things would get out of control.

All six sisters were together again for Sunday dinner. Helen did all the baking, cleaning, and preparation for the cooking. She was the best cook. Clora was always curious about Helen's weird behavior in the kitchen—eyes gleaming and refused help from the girls to cook in the kitchen. Who would be that happy to prepare so much food without help? Clora enjoyed watching Helen and Keeping her company while sitting at the kitchen table by the window. Diana, Shelia, and Renita were in the living room having drinks.

Brenda was quiet and ready to have the baby. Jesse Lyn was in another world, high as a kite. Clora's husband preferred to sit on the porch. He came into the house when dinner was served. All the sisters were envious of Clora once they were drunk or high on drugs. They were under the impression she had all of their parent's attention and love, though Jesse and Helen loved all their daughters. The sisters believed her green eyes and pretty looks were the reason. All five girls loved and resented Clora. Growing up as a child, she tried her best to obey her parents. The sisters caused her so much pain while growing up, not going to school and church. Clora always thought, in her heart, they were telling the truth. It was not her looks. She respected her parents and knew her place as a child. Her sisters were one of the reasons she wanted to get married so young. The family's name was a disgrace, and Clora was ashamed of her sisters' behavior. Her love for them was genuine. Mark was the love of her life and the knight coming to rescue his bride from the wicked sisters.

Brenda asked Clora to stay at her house a few days after the baby was born. Of course, Clora agreed to help her sister. Before dinner was over, the police were at the house for Diana. Jesse Lyn would not share her drugs with Diana, so a fight broke out between the two sisters. Diana had a knife. Dinner ended on a sour note as routine.

Two months later, Jesse Lyn and Diana told Helen they were pregnant. Things were happening at a fast pace for the family. Helen was raising one granddaughter, plus two more granddaughters were due in October just one week apart.

Brenda's baby was due in December on Christmas Day. Meanwhile, Clora was packing her clothes and thinking about missing her husband. She promised to spend a few days with the new baby and Brenda. Mark was proud of his wife and very protective. She was not worldly like her sisters.

This would be the first time apart since their marriage. A malicious act took place, or was it planned deliberately out of envy? The plot happened soon as Clora left her house. The truth came later. It changed lives forever, and people were seriously hurt.

Chapter 3

IN 1973, Shelia's son was born and Renita had a girl. Clora and Mark's son was born In January, the next year. Mark was a welder, and Clora was working nights at a nursing home. With this schedule, their son didn't go to daycare. Mark and his wife were very happy. Diana was forging checks to support her drug habit and making everybody's life miserable. Same story with Diana—another baby with medical problems and back in court for criminal acts. Her sentence was three years in the big house.

Jesse Lyn and her baby moved in with our mother. Their father was still busy with his life and the women of the night. Helen waited patiently for Jesse to come home sitting in her favorite chair by the front door. Clora always visited her mother and drove her to the grocery store. Helen wanted her daughter to have a better life and be independent. Clora thought Helen looked like a lost and frightened child. She did not like to see the sad look in her mother's eyes—such a beautiful lady.

She knows how to make her smile. *"Mother, remember when I was a little girl on my way to school. If I forgot to kiss you, I would run back home and you would be waiting at the decor for me."* Her mother knew she would run back home; the kiss made Clora happy.

The situation was too much for Helen. Three granddaughters and two worthless drug addict daughters with no jobs. Clora had to figure out a solution to help Helen. She took her niece home and took care of the child. She fell in love with the baby.

Things were quiet for a while and all the sisters were busy. Diana made parole. The next day, she was In rage and stormed over to Clora's apartment and accused her of stealing her daughter. There was no reasoning with this woman, a tormented soul, and a hollow heart. *"What went wrong?"* Clora politely told Diana to give her fifteen minutes to pack the baby's clothes and gave Diana the car seat. It was a sequence of events.

Brenda left her husband and daughter. She wanted to be a pole dancer and make money. Shelia's husband returned home from Vietnam and found out the boy was not his child.

Renita decided she was not ready to be a mother and gave her daughter to Helen. She chose to participate in a world of drugs, prostitution, and abuse with her daughter's father. Renita's boyfriend was selling drugs. A man broke into the apartment looking for drugs and money. Renita was shot in the back of the neck. Her boyfriend was killed.

Shelia in the meantime was broke and was put out of her apartment with nowhere to go. Of course, she thought of Clora's house to visit for a meal to eat and rest. Her sister welcomed them into her home. Shelia wandered from one place to another and was sleeping in different hotels with her son. Jesse got tired of Shelia and her son hanging out at the pool hall.

Next step, Shelia met Willie, a married man. His wife felt sorry for Shelia and her son because they were homeless. She and her husband could not have children. The lady moved them into her home, a major mistake. To make the long story short, Shelia slept with the woman's husband. The wife left Willie, which was probably Shelia's plan.

Jesse Lyn, Diana, Brenda, and Renita were out of control with sex, drugs, and fast money.

Helen was raising Mary, Lulu, and Patricia. Robin was left with Diana's husband most of the time. Brenda left her daughter Niki with her daddy's mother.

Clora was having her own personal! problems. Mark was a hard worker with issues. After being exposed to plenty of drama with Clora's sister, Mark was obsessed with his wife and wanted to know her every move and whereabouts at all times—extremely Jealous and violent. Praying was the only peace. Her only joy was her son. Clora was in the kitchen cooking, enjoying a quiet day at home.

Diana was trying to get away from her husband. He was beating her in the parking lot. The sisters lived in the same complex. The tenant downstairs knocked on Clora's door. The lady told her Diana was in trouble and needed help.

Clora went outside to check on her sister. While she was talking to her sister's husband, Diana ran upstairs looking like a madwoman in the apartment, and took the gun out of her sister's closet. The husband followed her to the apartment and said, *"Diana, don't try anything."*

It was too late; her mind was already made up. He was shot one time with a bullet in the heart and died. With Diana having Warrants, she ran and told her sister to get in the car. Clora had seen her sister as a stranger and was disturbed by Diana's actions. While they were in the car heading to Helen's house, Diana suddenly stopped the car and told her sister, *"Let's go back to your apartment."*

Trembling, Clora asks her sister, *"Are you going to call the police?"* Diana thought, *"How stupid you are, to make sure he is dead."* *"That is not a good ideal, Diana."* *"Just take me to Mother's house please."* She was ready to get rid of Clora. *"I will drop you off and keep rolling. Make sure you let Mother know I was tired of his abuse, OK?"*

Later, Diana called her father and told him about her whereabouts. She was hiding at a hotel. He gave the information to the police. Diana held a grudge against Jesse.

That was a long night, so I slept at my mother's house. Diana had to serve some years. Mother had four granddaughters to send to school. My mother and I were still very close and had our girl talks. She was getting tired so fast at the age of fifty-five.

Jesse was still at the pool hall. Brenda was on the north side of town doing her thing. She was snorting cocaine and dancing. Shelia was partying with Renita and staying out all night, and her son was left with his stepfather. Shelia and Renita visited me early one morning. They always waited for Mark to leave for work. They talked a lot about family stuff. Clora enjoyed cooking and having girl talk with her sisters. The sisters went back in time.

Jesse Lyn tripped out. She was hanging out with a woman that dressed like a dude. The chick walked and talked like a man. This went on for a while. Brenda acted like the singer James Brown—wore his hairstyle and danced like the man. The sisters were laughing so hard..

Tears were in their eyes. Shelia got jokes. She gave Renita the name Alfred. Stupid Renita thought that was a cool name, sucking her thumb.

Shelia told Renita the haircut made her look like a little boy. They had fun.

The hours went fast, and Mark would be home soon. They asked Clora to go to the club and have some drinks with them. Shelia called Clora a wimp and a fool for Mark. Her sister called her husband horrible names and a pothead. Clora never knew Mark smoked marijuana. Clora would always tell Mark her whereabouts. She did not have his permission. She was afraid to upset Mark. Renita decided to mess up her sister's world and mental state of mind. Why do her sisters have to ruin a good day? Renita said if Mark hit her one more time, she would tell his dirty secret. Of course, Shelia drilled Renita for details. Renita was waiting for a chance to let it out. She thought this was the perfect moment. *"Clora, the time you went to help Brenda with Niki, I had sex with Mark and he said he loves me."* Clora was dumbfounded and shocked—right under her nose. Shelia never did like him anyway. She always thought something was wrong with his behavior, and he was not good enough for her sister. Shelia took charge and told Clora to get dressed, and she knew a babysitter.

The sisters rode in Clora's car because they do not drive.

Later that night, Clora went home with a headache from drinking Tom Collins. As soon as she opened the door, Mark grabbed her by the arm.

She kept walking to the bedroom to lay their son in his bed. Clora let Mark know Renita told her all the details about their affair and his pot-smoking. He denied the affair and called her sister dirty names, angry because he got busted. Mark admitted the pot-smoking was true. Clora believed her sisters. What hurt the most, he did not apologize to her. That night, she told him to pack a bag and leave. Since Clora was the manager of the apartment, he left.

Chapter 4

THE PAIN was a heavy burden for Clora to carry. Clora found Mark's pot and took a few hits off the joint. She did not like the odor and flushed the joint down the toilet. Clora went back in time. In high school, she would see Mark, Renita, and the other kids standing in the hallway, the group that skipped class. All the boys liked her in school. Renita was not popular or smart. Her sister had a big crush on Mark. When Mark and Clora started dating, Renita was jealous. In her mind, her sister stole her boyfriend. Mark got caught in Renita's web. Clora looked forward to dressing up and looking pretty. Her new life consisted of going to the clubs. She met a man, but still had a love for Mark.

Her mother disapproved of David. Clora had feelings for the man and enjoyed his company.

Helen wanted her back with Mark. Two years later, Clora was pregnant with her second son. Mark was stalking her and sleeping with Renita for information on his wife. One day, the truth would be told to her son.

Today she would go outside. Clora was sitting on the porch at her mother's house, and Mark pulled up in the driveway. He got cut off the car and sat next to Clora.

They had small talk. Mark told Clora it was not important if the child was his or not. He made a lot of mistakes and loves his family. Mark told Clora he wanted his wife and son back. She did not answer Mark, and he left. Clora told her mother everything that was discussed. Clora did not trust Mark and was not ready to reconcile. Her mother knew with two children, it was not easy, and felt Clora's pain. In Helen's mind, she knew her daughter had nowhere to live. She did not like

Mark mistreating her. She wanted a better life for Clora. Her beautiful special child that brought her smiles was different. On this particular day, Clora saw her mother with different eyes. Helen was going against her religion. Her daughter did not agree and let Helen know. Clora was standing up for what she was taught and believed. Five of Helen's daughters were a disappointment, and she had high expectations for Clora.

Without saying a word, Clora saw the look in her mother's eyes. She said the words, "It is time to go home."

Mark was glad to hear Clora's decision. He said, "See you in twenty minutes."

Being the obedient daughter, she swallowed her pride and went to make a life with Mark once again. Before leaving, her mother said, "Remember your children will not always stay babies."

Clora was happy with doing the right thing. Mothers can always sense danger before it happens.

Renita was in the hospital three days later, badly beaten by one of her tricks. Clora rushed to the hospital to see her baby sister. It was hard to look at Renita with her face swollen like a pig. Clora could feel her sister's pain.

Clora told her sister no matter what happened, she would always love her. She felt that way about all her sisters because, in her way, she pitied them. Growing up was a childhood in perfect balance for Clora. She was Mary in the Christmas play in school, a cheerleader, Thomas Edison in a school play, an honor student, a volunteer at the nursing home, active in church, and starred in the play The Sky is the Limit, and that stuck with her through life. Her parents played a big part in her life. There are no perfect people in life, and she accepted them for who they are. Clora takes one day at a time. To Clora, being a mother is a gift and a blessing. She will love and protect her babies.

Renita was out of the hospital, the same lifestyle, dating men for money to score drugs. She would not take time to visit her daughter. When Clora's second son was born, Mark was mean and put on a different face around people. Clora's family had their own opinion of him. Mark saw himself as a rational man. He was self-righteous, accepting of Clora and her son. Mark and Clora were separated when she became pregnant. She intended to never go back to her husband.

15

Mark decided the biological father could not see the child. He would raise the boy as his son. Clora's sons mean the world to her. She buried her pain in prayer.

She got a call from her mother, asking her to come by the house. Brenda and Jesse Lyn went out to the club last night. Jesse Lyn was acting strange and refused to change her clothes. The behavior escalated; she closed all of the blinds, thinking someone was watching her, and locked the doors. Jesse was paranoid.

Helen was frightened. She called for help, 911. Jesse Lyn was taken away kicking, crying, and screaming. A straitjacket was placed on her arms.

Poor Brenda was scared thinking it was her fault, maybe someone slipped a mickey in Jesse's drink at the bar. Clora never believed that story. Shelia was still fighting with Willie and staying out late. Packing for a moving company was the only work she did. Shelia's husband got her the job.

Time for Diane to be released from prison again. Renita's time at the big house.

She was writing hot checks to buy drugs. Renita was sentenced to two years in prison. Her daughter was a big girl. Clora felt sorry for her nieces and spent time with them. They craved their mother's love and attention. This was getting old and tiresome because most of the time, Clora drove her mother all over Texas. She needed to find an outlet to get through all of this chaos. Diana was still an outlaw, just didn't know how to stay out of the cage. Jesse Lynn came home from the hospital. She lived with Helen. Clora put the thought of pot out of her mind. Jesse Lyn had many appointments. Helen went to the social security office. Jesse Lyn's social security number came up blank. The girl never had a job. She was able to receive a supplement check for mental illness. Clora found out the truth. Jesse Lyn's medical file read schizophrenia disorder.

Schizophrenia is caused by a chemical imbalance in the brain and environment, Antipsychotics are drugs to treat the symptoms. There is no cure. Medicine manages the symptoms. Negative symptoms, losing interest in everyday activities, such as bathing, grooming, or getting dressed. Feeling out of touch with other people, family, or friends. Lack of feeling or emotion.

Jesse Lyn went back to the hospital for a shock treatment. Helen never told her daughters the reason for Jesse Lyn's behavior. She lived in the backroom for many years.

Clora decided to go back to college, the only challenge she enjoyed, using her brain constructively and being exposed to a different environment, surrounded by positive people.

The sisters chose to be closed-minded. The mother went to Dr. Martin for a checkup and was told to take care of herself before she has a heart attack. Jesse called the sisters and set up a family meeting. The six sisters were present at their parent's house.

The meetings always took place at the kitchen table. Jesse gave his speech about the family pulling together. The sisters needed to make a better life and stop using drugs. It is time to take responsibility and raise their children. Jesse Lyn and her daughter had nowhere to live. Diana's oldest daughter lived with their mother since birth.

Shelia had her family, Brenda had her apartment, and Clora was dealing with Mark.

Renita's daughter was living with Helen. The sisters' wished things were normal. Diana did not want to hear what Jesse had to say. He was accountable for his actions. The old grudge came back. Revenge raced through her mind. Out of nowhere, Diana attacked her father, fighting and scratching Jesse in his face. The sisters stopped Diana and made her leave the house. Helen took Jesse to their room. Outbursts like this were no surprise to the sisters. Diana invented turmoil.

Brenda was ready to make a change. She thought the time was on her side. Brenda decided to put school on the back burner for one more year. The truth be told, she enjoyed dancing. Fast money became an addiction. Brenda sent her ex-mother-in-law money to take care of her daughter. She moved closer to her mother's house and helped Helen with her nieces. The arrangement did not last very long. Shelia caught her ex-husband coming out of Brenda's apartment.

She was furious after riding the bus on a hot summer day. The truth came out about Brenda and Melvin. The affair did not last very long. Shelia thought Brenda was using Melvin to buy furniture for her apartment. This was not the only reason Shelia had hatred in her heart.

Shelia was bitter for many years. Clora could not understand carrying the torch and pain that long. Every year, Shelia still talked about that day. Brenda thought it would be for the best to move to another part of town for good. After dancing for fourteen years, Brenda was ready to spend time with her daughter. Necole went to live with Brenda.

Diana got married to her third husband. She liked this husband because he used drugs.

Jesse Lyn was taking her medication. She was coming out of her room and sitting with the family.

Clora and Mark were still married. Their boys were older. The boys were close to Clora. They loved both their parents.

Clora had jobs in the medical field and the school district for six months at a time. Every time, Mark thought she was happy working and meeting people. He was not in control of his wife. In her husband's mind, his wife's place was at home with the boys. Clora was dealing with her pain and issues behind closed doors. There Was no one to talk to within the Miller clan, which is Mark's family. They have respect for one another, for the boys' sake. Behind Clora's back, Mark's mother called her an overprotective mother and a crazy Frenchman. Brown-skinned and dark-skinned people did not like pale-skinned people. That did not bother Clora. She experienced name-calling in school because of her green eyes and light skin.

Her mother-in-law made it understood, right or wrong, that she would stand by her son.

The first time Clora laid eyes on Mark; her life changed. She was so naive and innocent. Whatever words came out of his mouth, she used to believe him.

Mark was a truck driver, and she stayed at home with the boys. Her husband did not go to church with his family. Mark's childhood was not very good. His family was dysfunctional. Clora could not believe the behavior of Mark's mother. Mark's mother shot her husband in the leg. Dorothy was leaving for the weekend to meet her boyfriend. He was waiting in the car at their house. Grover was blocking the doorway, trying to stop his wife. Dorothy took him to the hospital.

Mark grew up watching his father work hard to give his mother cars, Jewels, clothes, new furniture, a pretty house, and money. She was the total opposite of Helen. Clora always made excuses for Mark's violent behavior. After so much abuse, her self-esteem was low. She would overheat. She was determined to find a solution to her problems. Her faith and belief were strong.

Shelia and Clora lived close to Helen's house. Driving over to Helen's house gave her time to think. She refused to live her life like Helen. Her mother was the love of her life. Clora's mother did the best she knew how to raise the girls. Her advice was not always right. Clora understood people make bad choices and mistakes. Telling her daughter to overlook Mark's actions and tolerate abuse because she has children and a husband that provides for his family. Clora's poor mother was confused and wrapped up in living her life for Jesse. She lost or no longer knew her identity. Helen was tired and unhappy over the years. Giving up the strength to fight back is like suicide. One day, sitting at the kitchen table drinking coffee, Clora asks Helen what happened to her girls. Her mother blamed each sister for making bad choices. She thought the sisters were weak, and Clora was the strong link. That was not the answer Clora wanted to hear. Helen was never big on discussing family problems. She was a complex woman at times. Maybe she did not want to talk about the truth, was in denial, or was clueless.

Diana picked up Renita from the bus station, and they got high. Diana knew the state released ex-convicts with one hundred dollars.

The sisters and their families were preparing for Thanksgiving dinner. Clora was up early that day preparing breakfast for her sons and husband.

She told Mark to meet her at Helen's house later. When she looked at her husband, Clora did not know if her feelings for Mark were pity or love.

Helen was happy to see Clora. No one else could help cook in her kitchen but Clora. There was plenty of food, cakes, and pies. The six sisters were together again. The sisters made a pack not to live Helen's life and not with a man like Jesse. Jesse Lyn and her daughter, Diana and her two daughters, Brenda and her daughter, Shelia and her son, Clora and her two sons, and Renita with her daughter. Mark, Willie, and Lee, the sons-in-law. This was the first holiday in a very long time that things were going OK, enjoying dinner with laughter, joy, and family love.

After everyone left and went home to their house, Clora helped clean the kitchen and house. Helen looked tired, so Clora told Jesse the girls were going home with her and spending the night. When Clora left the house, Helen was sitting in her favorite chair with the bible.

The kids stayed up and watched television for a while. My niece said, *"Aunt Clora, did you hear someone knocking at the door?"*

Clora said yes and went to answer the door. No one was outside. Clora knew there was a knock. Fifteen minutes later, her house phone was ringing.

She answered the phone, and her mother's neighbor Mrs. Lola told her to come to Helen's house as fast as she could.

Clora was told Helen was having a heart attack. She, Mark, and the children left the house quickly. Mark was driving the car and sped with caution to the house of Clora's mother. She got out of the car running to the scene. The ambulance was there with Helen on the stretcher.

She rode in the back of the ambulance with her mother. Helen was announced dead on arrival at the hospital. Cause of death—myocardial.

A heart attack is the interruption of blood supply to a part of the heart, causing heart cells to die. Symptoms: sudden chest pain radiating to the left arm or left side of the neck, palpitations, sweating.

There was no family history of heart attacks. Helen did have severe headaches. She took medication for migraine. Migraine is a chronic neurological disorder characterized by moderate to severe headaches. Affecting one-half of the head can last up to seventy-two hours.

She also took medicine for asthma. Asthma is a common chronic inflammatory disease of the airways—airflow constriction and broncho-spasm. Symptoms include wheezing, coughing, tightening of the chest, and shortness of breath.

Clora reminisced about when she was ill as a child. Helen gave her special attention. Clora had asthma at a very young age. Her mother would rub her chest with Vicks VapoRub. The medicine was strong for her nose and eyes. The warm towel on her chest felt good. Helen was so gentle and caring. She was very protective. Helen did not want Clora to help the sisters with housework because of the dust. The sisters' thought Helen was overreacting. Memories she would always cherish.

Shelia was the first sister Clora saw at the hospital. Their mother was fifty-eight years old, and she was aged ten. Shelia suffered from migraine headaches.

Chapter 5

CLORA WAS TWENTY-EIGHT YEARS OLD. She and Helen were both too young to be without each other. So much joy that morning and pain in the night. Helen's wish was to be cremated, but that did not happen. Clora wanted her mother's wish to be respected. She knew it was best not to argue with Diana. Jesse was grieving. All the guilty sisters started taking charge. The funeral service was held at St. Frances Catholic Church. All the girls had their First Communion at the church.

It Was a very sad occasion. Clora was upset because all her sisters had a part in their mother's heart attack. The burden of raising girls again was a heavy load. Each sister dealt with the death of Helen and their grief differently. The family served dinner at Jesse's house after the funeral service.

Mrs. Iola, the next-door neighbor, said Helen was at peace. Helen was a proud woman and did not talk about her problems with Mrs. Iola. The old lady could see and hear the turmoil that took place next door. Jesse went straight to his room. Two years before his wife's death, he sold the pool hall and spent time with her. The sisters did not understand the kind of love Jesse and Helen shared. They always felt the love Helen had for Jesse. He did not show his affection to his wife in front of the girls. No hugs and kisses, only the words *"I love you."*

The house was filled with family and friends. The neighbors adored Helen's sweet personality and at the same time sympathizing with her situation. Raising six girls was not an easy task.

Clora went to check on her father in his room. The door was locked, and she heard him crying. In the front part of the house, she could hear crying and laughter.

Jesse Lyn did not have much to say and went to her room after dinner. Diana had to put on a fake performance. She was self-destructive with no remorse. Helen told the sisters Diana made her nervous coming by the house on drugs. We never found out why Diana was full of rage. Brenda was still dancing—a daughter with a big heart when she had money. The memory that she kept of Helen helped her in life. Her mother took the time to teach Brenda how to talk. She had a speech problem.

Shelia was mean and sass to Helen. She was always in trouble. They were two of a kind, controlling personalities. Shelia wanted more love from Helen and felt cheated.

Clora remembered the good times growing up with Helen. She was called Helen's shadow. At three years old, she followed Helen's every footstep. Growing up as a child was easy because she knew not to be rebellious. She always smiled and said yes, mother.

Renita sucked her thumb all the time. Helen was always worried about her. She could have been a sweet person but chose not to be. In reality, they were six lost sisters without Helen. No matter how they fought or disagreed, she taught them to always be there for one another. In all of their turmoil, the six sisters were very protective of each other. In no time, Diana and Renita were running buddies. Brenda went back to her lifestyle. Shelia and Clora would help Jesse with Diana's two daughters, Jesse Lyn's one daughter, and Renita's one daughter. All the grandchildren were of school age. Mary, the oldest of the girls, combed their hair and helped clean the house. Jesse was a good cook. When the bills had to be paid every month, Clora wrote the checks for her father. His wife was in charge of all the paperwork. His reading was very limited. In the meantime, Clora had Mark and her two sons to take care of.

The first Christmas without Helen was heartbreaking. Brenda gave Jesse and her nieces their presents on Christmas Eve and spent Christmas with her daughter. Jesse Lynn, Diana, Shelia, and Renita helped Jesse with the decorations and cooking.

Clora had Christmas at her mother-in-law's house. Later that evening, Mark drove her to Jesse's house to drop off presents.

Shelia, Renita, and Diana were drunk and talking loudly. Clora.

wished everyone a Merry Christmas.

She could not wait to get out of the house, Sheila said, *"Bye, Mrs. Goody Two-Shoes."* Diana's speech was slurring. "Clora and her little family are too good to spend Christmas with us."

Jesse told the sisters to be quiet. Renita said, *"You are always taking up for her."*

Clora went to Jesse Lyn's room, and she was asleep. This was the perfect time to leave.

In the summer, of 1985, Jesse decided it was time for Jesse Lyn and her daughter to move to an apartment. Daddy gave her a shock treatment with his speech. Diana helped Jesse find the apartment two streets from his house. The sisters knew Jesse was capable of living on her own. The doctor told Helen as long as Jesse Lyn took her medication every day, she would be able to take care of herself. Diana thought Jesse Lyn was selfish and used her mother.

Growing up, Diana and Jesse Lyn did not like each other. They never connected as sisters. Diana was Daddy's girl, and Jesse Lynn was her mother's girl. Diana resented Helen. In her mind, her mother made a difference with the sisters. Clora did not believe that was the truth; Diana was jealous of her sister.

Jesse Lyn and her daughter were doing well. The school was across the street.

Diana married a merchant seaman the same year. Countee bought her a new house, car, Jewels, furniture, mink coat, and a grocery store. One of the daughters went to live with Diana and her husband.

Mary was attending high school. Her granddaddy's house was her only home since birth.

Renita was not stable. She was visiting her daughter and father weekly.

One year later, Diana asked Clora to work at her store. She taught her sister everything about the business. Her husband was always reading magazines about the rich and famous. Countee did not know how to work the cash register, which lames to the business.

After three months passed, Diana was restless with the store. That was not good. She told Clora she needed a vacation. She wanted her sister to open and close the store. Clora was supposed to watch Countee with the money. One week passed by and no Tiana. The trip was scheduled for a few days.

Clora knew her sister was on a drug spree.

Diana called the store the next day, desperate for money, asking her sister to put the store's money in a bank bag. When her husband left the store to call her, Clora told Diana no. She was not getting involved with stealing money. Diana began raging and told her to leave the store and not to come back.

Clora locked up the store and went home. Mark was sick of the drama. His wife's sisters needed to handle their problems. He wanted control of Clora. Her husband would rather work than spend time with his family. In his mind, she was another Helen. A doormat for him and the children. What little did he know? Clora's faith and belief were strong. Jesus gave her the strength to hold on. Clora was good at finding vocational programs for people with low income.

Jesse was still dating Maybelle, before and after his wife's death. The six sisters understood their father needed a companion.

Jesse never remarried because of his love and devotion to Helen's memories.

Diana's marriage was over. Her other daughter was back living at Jesse's house.

Clora's boys were growing fast.

They were ten and seven years old. She had enough time to drop the boys off at school. The house was clean and dinner would be ready before the boys and Mark came home. Her husband was satisfied with the arrangements. Clora was content and studied hard to make high scores.

Evelyn was her study partner. She liked to challenge Clora with law research. Those were the good days.

Mark came to his wife's graduation. Clora locked for Evelyn and did not see her.

She hoped her friend did not drink too much gin last night. Evelyn and Clora were announced for perfect attendance and honor awards. Clora received her paralegal certificate. She called Evelyn, but there was no answer. It was like her friend vanished. They shared some happy times.

Mark looked forward to Clora waiting on him and the nchildren again.

Diana and Renita were strung out on heroin, needle marks all over their bodies.

Daddy's health was poor. There were days his legs hurt. Jesse had gout, and it caused his legs to swell with pain. Gout is a medical condition usually characterized by recurrent attacks of acute inflammatory arthritis—a red, tender, hot, swollen joint.

Diana was sick with a nasty cough. Clora took her to the hospital. She needed an IV for body fluids. The doctor took one look at Clora's sister and was frustrated. The doctor did not see a vein. All of Diana's veins collapsed. The needle had to go in her neck. Clora was embarrassed for both of them. The hospital kept Diana for several days.

Mary was Diana's oldest daughter. She did not need her mother's blessing. She went to the courthouse and married Derrick. She was living with her grandfather while her husband served in the army.

Renita was missing for days at a time. She had not bathed and showed up at Jesse's house dirty and hungry.

While Diana was in the hospital, the nurse drew her blood. Diana has tuberculosis with HIV coinfection. Her CD4 count was less than two hundred cells. AIDS is a disease of the human immune system caused by the human immunodeficiency virus (HIV}.

Renita visited Diana at the hospital. She told Renita to get her blood test. Renita's blood test was positive for HIV. This condition progressively reduces the effectiveness of the immune system and leaves individuals susceptible to opportunistic infections and tumors. Thank God Helen is not here to see this nightmare.

Diana and Renita did not change, using drugs and spreading the virus. They were killing machines. The two of them infected many lovers and husbands. Clora had to wire money to Renita, stranded in Austin, Texas. She broke her leg, and the doctor put a cask on it. The man left town without her. She was staying at Clora's house until the paperwork was completed.

The state-approved her check and apartment. Same procedure for Diana.

Jesse's health was declining. He was in and out of the VA hospital.

There's nothing more the hospital could do for Jesse and sent him home.

Brenda did not come around very much. She was afraid of all the sickness. Shelia and her husband were busy working out of town.

Jesse Lynn still walked over to her daddy's house. All the people in the community knew she begged for cigarettes. They did not bother her, calling Jesse Lyn the crazy lady. Somedays Jesse Lyn stopped taking her medication.

Renita's daughter was pregnant at thirteen. Her father's mother took the girl to live with her.

Mark was drinking beer and chasing women. He encouraged Clora to help her family. She was not able to see his actions. His wife was too busy with her sisters.

The truth about Mark came later. Diana met husband number 3 at the HIV clinic. Diana and Murphy moved in with Jesse and took poor care of him. Both of Diana's daughters were pregnant. The girls did not want to live with Diana and moved into their apartment. Diana and Murphy were violent people.

The sisters visited their father and made sure he is OK. Diana always made the visits to the house unpleasant for her sisters.

Jesse Lynn's daughter was pregnant. She stopped taking her medication again, and Diana drove Jesse Lyn to the hospital. Diana found out her sister has schizophrenia. Helen never told the other sisters.

Clora kept quiet at her mother's request. Diana drove Jesse Lyn home. The hospital changed her medication. Instead of being nice to her sister, Diana was mean.

The minute she walked into her father's house; she was making jokes about her sister's illness to her husband. She made sure the sisters were aware of what took place at the hospital.

As time went on, Jesse Lyn met a man at the store. She was able to cope with dating and helping her daughter.

Clora always forgave Mark's infidelity and focused on her boys. Her husband was in and out of jail for traffic tickets. She had to bail him out. Mark always thought his family had sense and class. His wife's family was lunatics and trash. Well, he was disappointed.

His mother divorced her husband and married her lover. The oldest brother was an alcoholic and gay.

The oldest sister had a nervous breakdown and called everyone demons. She carried holy water in her purse. The other sister went from a pothead to a crackhead. The youngest sister wrote hot checks and had a gambling addiction. The youngest brother was using heroin.

Clora and Mark were spending more time with their sons. He was loving his wife.

Their bond was very strong. They needed each other as a family. On good days, Mark promises his wife a new home and new car. She did not stay angry with him very long. The sisters always made jokes about her old house, old car, old furniture, and old clothes. Clora was a good homemaker. The old house was always clean, the boys were well groomed for school, and they always had food on the table.

Chapter 6

IN **1989.** Jesse died at the hospital from chronic illness. Gout caused high uric acid levels in the blood.

Clora and her family attended the funeral services.

When she visited Jesse at the hospital, he was in high spirits. He told Clora it was time to be with Helen. She smiled and told him to say hi to her. That's the memory Clora would keep of Jesse.

The five sisters went to Jesse's house after the service. Bertha, his insurance agent, knew the family for two decades. The sisters wanted to know about the policy. They were in a rage to hear Clora was the beneficiary. Brenda asked if they could cash the policy without me.

Bertha explained this was a legal document for Clora. She came to Clora's house the next day.

Clora was not surprised by their behavior. After the funeral expenses, the balance was five thousand dollars. That gave the sisters another reason to resent her. When her mother passed, the sisters took all her belongings. Jesse saved Helen's pearl necklace for her. Shelia needed a ride to the attorney's office and asked Clora to pick her up. In the will, she was the executive of the house. She was upset and told Clora to take the will home. The old house had to be remodeled and left to the six girls. Renita's daughter was living at the house and pregnant.

The house could be sold after she was eighteen years old.

Another shock for the sisters, Clora looked pregnant. Renita and Shelia said she was too old. Clora's two sons were happy about the new addition to the family. Junior was sixteen years old, and Tony was thirteen.

Mark took his wife to the doctor in October for a checkup. She missed her monthly cycle. They were tickled and surprised. The baby was due in July 1989. Mark was working hard and spending time with his family.

Brenda changed her lifestyle and went to community college. She was thirty-six years old and working at the homeless shelter.

Shelia was having problems with her husband.

Jesse Lyn was busy with her grandchildren and boyfriend.

Renita's boyfriend moved into her apartment. The Sunday dinners were no longer at the family's house. Jesse Lyn was in the habit of walking to the house. Diana and her husband were sick most of the time.

Brenda, Shelia, and Clora were not comfortable visiting Diana with Murphy at the house. They were two of a kind—drugs, partying, fighting, profanity, and stealing.

The sisters visit Renita. She has a big heart with no brain.

Clora's son was now one year old. She would remember this day for the rest of her life.

Mark came home from work and walked into the bedroom. His wife had gained weight and felt depressed. He told Clora, two days earlier, more women to love with all that meat.

She asked her husband if he had a good day.

Mark put his hand on the back of her neck and said, *"Look at you. Meat on the back of your neck, just like your daddy."*

Clora could not understand why he was being so cruel. Mark thought of every fat name to say. Called the sisters and her worthless. Told Clora it was her fault. He slept with her sister. She would not give him oral sex. Clora was a virgin with no experience.

In time, maybe his wife would have tried different positions in the bedroom. Mark blew that opportunity with Clora, and she never changed her mind. The baby was asleep. She went outside to check on the other boys. Clora refused to let Mark see her cry and held the pain in, nor argue with him.

When Mark and the boys left the house the next morning, his wife cried and ask God for help. Her self-esteem was very low. The next month, she called Mary, the oldest niece, and asked for a ride to the hospital. Clora checked herself into the psychiatric ward.

The psychologist did an evaluation. Dr. Stien confirmed what Clora already knew. The doctor explains the result to her and said, *"You are highly intelligent. There is no need for medication. I can schedule an appointment if you would like to talk."*

Her niece thought she was tripping. Clora explained to her niece, *"It takes a smart person to seek help or advice."*

On the way home, she thought about her mother. Clora was determined to break the cycle. This journey was going to take time. Growing up, Clora had only two mirrors to look at in Helen's house. She did not want to wear her mother's shoes. Her sisters did not know how to live. God cannot do the work for her by himself. Clora was ready to do her part.

Mark was curious about her conversation with the doctor and accused Clora of telling a stranger his business. Clora kept her appointment. One session changed her life for the better.

All the pain she held in was released. Clora talked about Mark and Renita betraying her trust. Mark never admitted he was wrong, always blaming her sisters. Mark abused her emotionally and physically. The expectations Helen set. Crying was the way to let her pain out and express what she felt. Clora knew Mark needed therapy.

Clora took a giant step, and this was just the beginning for her. Mark refused help, afraid that some people would find out the truth.

Shelia's husband was smoking crack cocaine. Their packing business was losing clients.

The delivery truck with the furniture was never on time.

Mark and Clora were having a baby girl. Mark adores Michelle. Clora had surgery. Tubes were clipped at thirty-six years old.

Clora was focused on her family. Four children were depending on their mothers. The oldest son was seventeen, the next son was fifteen, the third son was two years old, and her daughter was six months.

In 1992, Clora's eldest son's high school called her to come to the principal's office. Panic set in her stomachache. Clora was rushing her son to the emergency clinic. A classmate took a combination lock and hit her son in the head. Clora always took action and stayed strong for the children in a crisis.

She could soothe their fear. The doctor took X-rays and gave the boy a shot. The hairline fracture would close. Clora was furious and thank God the principal kept her separated from the boy. Calming her son down was a hard task. He could take care of himself: fear caused this boy to overreact. Mark could not deal with certain situations.

Michelle was one year old, and her daddy refused to leave her side.

Shelia and her husband lost the packing business. After her son graduated from high school, she left Willie and moved to an apartment.

Clora's house was very busy. This summer, the second son was graduating from high school.

Tony was never a problem—very smart in school and always home on time. Clora's mother advised her to keep the truth a secret.

At the age of eighteen, Tony told his mother he felt different. It was time for Clora to sit down and listen to Tony. She knew exactly what he was trying to say and understood his feelings.

Clora and Mark already had this discussion. She would tell Tony the truth. Her son was dealing with his identity—opposite of his brother. Clora explained to Tony she was very happy when the pregnancy test results read positive. He was conceived from Clora and David's love. She wanted stability for both of her sons. Tony had tears in his eyes. He asked to meet David.

Mark agreed to let David visit Tony. Clora was afraid of losing her son to David.

After two days with David, Tony came home. His mother was happy and relieved.

Tony talked with his daddy and mother. He told Mark, *"You are the only father I love and know."* Tony decided not to visit David anymore; he was finding himself.

The two little ones were keeping their mother busy. Things were going Mark's way. He believed in keeping his family together. They were his strength.

The oldest son's girlfriend was pregnant with twins. Junior was disappointed because Nancy was not ready for another marriage. Her son was taught to do the right thing as a father. Six months after the twin boys were born, Clora's son was having headaches. She took Junior to the doctor for a checkup. Sinus was the cause for his head hurting. The medication was not working.

Clora was preparing dinner for her family, Mark, and the children.

As a mother, observation was very important with children.

She noticed Junior's forehead was protruding in two areas. Clora instantly examined the knots. This was not normal. Mark stayed at home with the kids.

Clora drove her son to the emergency room. Once the doctor saw the knots, Junior was taken to the examination room. Clora had to wait in the lobby. A team of doctors had a conference. The diagnosis was explained to her. The disease control and neurosurgeon were called to the hospital. Clora never left her son. Sinus infection caused the headaches. The infection was on the brain. The doctors told Clora they had never seen a case like this before.

In the first procedure, insert a large needle into his head to drain the greenish pus. Clora had to be very strong. She watched the needle fill up with pus. Only one knot went down. Next, Junior was on the stretcher sedated, then a CT scan and MRI of the head. Brain surgery was the only option to save her son's life. Clora took a few minutes to pray and call her husband. The doctor inserted a catheter in her son's head to remove and release residual pus. The second MRI was taken.

Mark was at the hospital with his wife. He did not know where his wife got so much strength from. He was hurting for his wife and son. Clora was not leaving the hospital. Mark went home and saw about the other children.

Two doctors talked with Clora. The abscess caused pus on the frontal lobe of the brain. The surgeons would drill his skull to scrape the frontal. Junior's head was open from the left ear across the top of the head to the right ear. The doctors came out of surgery to tell Clora it was a miracle. Her son is alive. Junior was moved to the intensive care unit. Clora was blessed, her son is alive. Tubes were everywhere and staples in his head from left to right. Her handsome son was disfigured and in severe pain. Her heart was full of love, and her eyes saw her baby, not a grown man. She was happy and tired.

After a few hours of sleep and she went back to the hospital. She had to be there when he woke up. The next morning, Mark went to the hospital with Clora. After a few minutes, he left the unit. Clora sat and talk with Junior until he fell asleep. ICU limit was twenty minutes for visitors.

During the weeks, Clora was spending time at the hospital. Mark and Tony took turns visiting Junior. They would go to work and come home. Tony had plenty of patience with his little brother and sister. Three days after the surgery, the hospital called Clora at home. She was informed of her son's condition. He refused to eat and was giving up the will to fight. Junior's favorite food was Clora's homemade SOLID.

She quickly prepared the soup and went to the hospital. The minute she walked into the room, Clora took her son's hand and prayed. He could hear his mother praying.

Clora looked up at her son and saw a smile on his face. Jesus answered her prayers. She fed him the homemade soup. Junior told his mother her soup always worked magic. Clora was happy and watched him fall asleep.

Junior was moved to a room four days later. His mother would not let her family or Mark's family visit. They were being nosy and gossiping too much. Junior was disoriented and had a head the size of a flying saucer. Mark's mother was upset and accused Clora of being overprotective. Her son was talking a lot, not with sense to her. His father thought the boy used too much profanity.

Tony talked about the twins growing fast. Tony loves his brother. Mark loves his son and feels helpless. His son was talking a lot with his mother. Mark noticed his son's behavior was strange. Nancy visited Junior, and she felt uncomfortable. The doctor scheduled Junior for sinus surgery, an incision under the eye-nasal process. The prefrontal cortex, the most anterior region of the brain, comprises several key areas that are important for higher mental functions that control human personality including anticipation and planning, memory judgment, and decision making. Damage or lesions to this region of the brain can result in major personality changes. Encephalitis (epilepsy) can cause frontal lobe seizures.

The nurse gave Clora boxes of medical supplies and instructions. Changing the bandages was a sterile procedure. The open wounds could not get infected. Clora devoted all her time and attention to nursing her son. The visiting nurse came to the house and checked Junior's progress. She was pleased with the care of his wounds. Clora's days consisted of being a nurse, wife, homemaker, and mother. She spent quality time with

Mark and each child.

Summer was next month. Six months since the surgery, Junior was getting restless. Junior was aware of the ugly scar and staple marks on his head. Clora kissed the top of her son's head. Junior was self-conscious of the scar and wished it would go away.

The sisters would call and ask how Junior was doing. The youngest sister came to Clora's house.

The children were not close to their grandmother. She never spent time with them.

Tony kept his brother up-to-date about the neighborhood. The youngest boy was going to school. Clora was babysitting the twins twice a week. Her daughter enjoyed playing with the boys. Junior's hair grew over the scar. He went walking in the neighborhood. Clora's world was turned upside down. She was driving the streets at night looking for her son. He was smoking pot and selling drugs, thinking everyone was his friend.

Mark loves his wife. He told her Junior was out of control.

It is time she took care of her health and the other children. The sisters have plenty of gossips. Michelle was of school age. Clora made an appointment for Junior.

The state doctor evaluated the boy and noticed a peculiar behavior. Told Clora, that her son did not qualify for social security, and the case closed. His mother only wanted medical treatment.

In 1996, Junior called his mother from the county Jail. He was caught selling drugs. Mark refused to get involved. He explained his love for all his children, and one child was not going to destroy the family. Clora went to court and hired a lawyer. After Mark and the children fell asleep, she would read her law books. Clora kept all her books from college.

Ignorance of the law is no excuse. In other words, the same law applied to everyone. Clora had the lawyer introduce her son's medical record and medication (Dilantin). Junior served one year in the medical ward.

Mark was beginning to relax with his family. Tony was concerned about his brother. AJ and Michelle were very close to Tony. He reminded his mother of Gentle Ben, six feet tall and weighing 218 8 pounds. A kind loving heart.

Mark promised to buy his wife a house.

He had an eighteen-wheeler and Clora budgeted money well. Since Mark was an independent driver and had low credit scores, he had a plan. His wife would work temporarily and her credit was good. Clora gave Mark a big hug and kiss. She went to the University of Houston for criminal justice. Clora was hired at Darrington Prison Unit, working nights as a correctional officer. Mark was in the habit of letting things go her way.

Clora heard so many horror stories about prison. She had to find out for herself. Maybe this would ease her stress. Mark and Clora had a beautiful two-story house built. Clora chose the floor plan and colors for the tile and carpet. Five months later, Mark insisted his wife stop working. Clora listened to her husband and quit the Job. The working conditions were poor. A horrible place to be, and she found the answers to her questions.

The next year, Junior was released from prison on parole. Mark hoped his son would do right. His father brought Junior his first car. His friend gave the boy a job at the grocery store.

Mark bought Tony a car for graduation. He went to ITT Tech with Tony and applied for financial aid. Mark was disappointed with his son's decision. Tony decided to wait a year. He went to work for National Car Rental. Mark, not having much education, wanted more for his sons. He did not have a role model growing up. He had no directions.

Junior was spending time with the family. Clora was happy. She knew it was not for very long. Her son's brain relearned or programmed one way. The street life of drugs and fast money. Mark got upset and told him no one wants to hear that trash. Clora changed the subject.

All her sisters except Diana visit the new house. Michelle had a birthday party. Mark and Clora's family came to the party. Junior was home for one year and went back to prison. Her son was the first grandchild in prison.

Jesse Lyn was better. Her daughter moved across the street with her children. Diana was spending lots of time at the hospital. Brenda was petting a government grant to buy a two-story house. Shelia found a two-story house for rent. Clora put money on the books and wrote letters to her son. Mark went with his wife to visit Junior. Tony brought a nice girl home to meet his parents. The school bus stops in front of house for AJ and Michelle. Clora volunteered for the kids' field trips. The school offered free computer classes for parents. Clora attended the class and received a computer certificate. It was fun learning with other moms. She never used a computer before.

Mark's old truck had broken down. He could no longer afford the repairs.

Mark needed his wife's help. He decided when his wife worked or stayed at home. Clora went to school for a few weeks. She passed the state test. The license was to work in Home Health Care. Maxim Healthcare Services hired Clora the next week.

The hours were perfect. The children's bus arrived at 7:30 a.m. She punched in at 8:00 a.m. Clora made it home thirty minutes before the bus. She had weekends and holidays off. Every other Saturday, her children and the grandsons went to Chunky Cheese, skating ring, movies, the mall, or play games at home. Mark would Join them some time; the holidays were a joyous occasion. Plenty of food and love.

Junior was in and out of his family's life. His mother would pray, visit, write letters, and put money on the books. Mark was getting fussy about the bills. Clora told Mark to buy a one-level house. He got smart and told her to believe in him. Mark liked to act out his anger. He wanted to hit Clora. That was not a good idea. She tried to cut his finger off with a knife. Mark improved his verbal skills. The sisters always stayed in touch, talking over the telephone.

Clora was pleased working for Dr. Gray; his personality is cheerful. Mark signed a lease-purchase plan with North American Van Lines. Diana's T-cell count dropped. She was using drugs and neglecting her appearance. Renita was spending less time with Diana. She was trying to kick drugs. Brenda was busy with her grandson. Shelia occupied her spare time with family gossip. Jesse Lyn had a home health provider. The six sisters took one day at a time.

Life was a roller coaster for Clora. Mark was not afraid of hard work. He never worked for a company for more than two years. He was a screwup. Mark wrecked the truck and went back to Laredo Construction. His pride was hurt.

Dr. Gray retired after Clora made one year on the job. She received unemployment checks. Clora paid her way through cosmetology school.

By this time, Mark was furious with his wife. Clora had a beauty shop. She liked the name Salon of Miracles. The sisters were surprised. Shelia, Renita, and Jesse Lyn were clients.

Brenda visited the shop periodically. Diana was resentful and never stepped foot in the shop. Mark wanted to be happy for Clora, but his ego was in the way. Clora leased the shop for three years. Laredo Construction signed a contract in the Bahamas. Mark was back in charge. Clora would not renew the lease and stay at home with the children. Mark and the children were very happy with the arrangement.

Shelia invited Renita and Clora to her house for lunch. Shelia's advice was never right. The lecture: mother is dead and it's time for Clora to live her life. When she was finished with Mark, he went from six feet tall to six inches. Renita made sure her glass was full of wine. Shelia would have you and your children living on the streets, sleeping with different men. In the end, a life living alone. Brenda thought Shelia had a negative attitude and a grudge against men. They were not very close. Shelia had her issues to work out. It was easy for Clora to make excuses for all her sister's behavior.

This way she was able to keep love in her heart for each sister. Meanwhile, the family's house needed to be repaired and taxes were delinquent. Clora arranged a plan for the back taxes.

Shelia, Brenda, Renita, and Jesse Lyn were not concerned with the taxes. They did not have any money to contribute to taxes. Diana called Clora on the telephone. She was deranged and accused her sister of taking the house. At the end of the conversation, she expressed hatred for Clora and told her, *"You are no longer my sister."* The virus was affecting Diana's brain. Her husband could no longer live with Diana's violent behavior. He had full-blown AIDS. Her two daughters were busy with their children. Less than a year later, Diana died of AIDS. The once beautiful swan turned into an ugly duckling.

The funeral was very small, and no one spoke on her behalf. Clora respected her sister's wish and did not attend the service.

She said a silent prayer for Diana. Clora remembered her sister was afraid of being happy. When things were good and she had a smile on her face, Diana would become self-destructive, like she thought it was not supposed to last. She did not believe people could change. Diana would not put trust in people or happiness, not wanting to be disappointed. Diana stopped looking at life sober at the age of fifteen.

Shelia's work was slow in the winter months. Her boyfriend moved in to help pay the bills. Shelia's son and his daughter lived at the house also. Brenda was divorcing her fifth husband. Jesse Lyn, on her good days, walks to the family's house and sits on the porch. The house was Vacant. She was aware the house was empty but felt close to her memories. Renita's daughter and grandchildren enjoyed listening to her jokes.

Clora had to put her fear aside and make a stand. Mark's job hired Tony to work on the barge in New Orleans. Tony wanted to make money to help support his son. He was bitter that his mother rejected his marriage proposal.

Brenda, Shelia, and Clora went to the hospital to visit Renita. Their baby sister was very sick. Renita told Clora to be happy, and she Was sorry for trying to steal her life. No one could stay angry long with Peanut. She had a peanut brain and a childlike mind. Renita's daughter took care of the funeral arrangements. Renita did not have a church home. 5t. John Church held the service. She visited the church before with her daughter. The four sisters, family, and friends remembered her smile. The casket was closed with her picture on top. The virus put years on her and changed her facial features. Everyone shared good memories of the funny jokes she told. Renita was forty-two years old. Diana was forty-six years old.

Jesse Lyn was using drugs and stopped taking her medication. Her daughter admitted her to the hospital. Jesse Lyn's only daughter had five kids. Renita's one daughter had five children. Diana's oldest daughter had two girls, and the youngest daughter had three children. Three of the nieces were getting public assistance.

Clora waited for her two children to fall asleep. She explained to her husband they had major problems in the marriage. She wanted the abusive pattern to change. The conversation was poling in circles.

Clora told Mark the plan. She was going back to work and moving to an apartment. The children deserved a healthy environment. Two loving parents that solved family problems without verbal abuse. Mark became very angry. He cried and promised to stop drinking.

A month later, Mark and the two children helped Clora move into her apartment. Mark and Clora explained to the children their parents needed time to work things out. They were still a family with lots of love. Mark and Clora talked every day on the phone. He asked Clora to go on a date. They went to dinner and the movies. Mark drank coffee with Clora at the apartment. They talked for hours.

Mark and the children were going to church on Sundays. Clora went to church with her family. Every other Sunday, Clora had to work. Those Sundays after work, she would cock dinner for her family. The children were happy to see their parents being nice to each other.

When the apartment was quiet and she was by herself, Clora used this time to pray and take a look at her faults. She had a vicious tongue. It was time for her to bury the past. Take responsibility for her actions. This was the first time Clora lived with independence. It was OK temporarily. Shelia was having issues with Rufus. He was rude and selfish with his money. Brenda and Shelia never agreed on any subject. Mark stopped drinking beer and admitted his mistakes. He apologized and asked for another chance. During those nine months apart, Mark and Clora had a lot to learn about themselves and each other. She was liking her husband's new ways. Clora told him not to get biblical in the bedroom.

In 2006, Mark and Clora renewed their marriage vows. At the church, the family became members. Thirty-four years of marriage and still loving each other. Clora kept working after moving back home. Mark spent time with AJ and Michelle.

Shelia was upset with Clora. She did not believe in love and happiness. The three sisters visited Jesse Lyn at the nursing home. Cigarettes and coke cans were at the top of her long list. She was meeting new friends. Jesse Lyn would always struggle with mental illness. She was safe and no dope here.

Mark was having financial problems. He was losing the house after ten years. Laredo was underbid for the Bahamas contract. His wife Was very calm about losing the house. Mark took the loss very hard and used all of his retirement, filed for bankruptcy and the mortgage payments doubled. The house went into foreclosure.

Shelia was at the hospital with Rufus. He had a bad liver and other chronic illneof having. together, Brenda

Brenda was dating a married man. He was an alcoholic.

41

She met him at the bar every day and drank.

Clora and Mark found a house together and a better school district for the children. Clora was teaching preschoolers at a daycare. On holidays and birthdays, the three sisters have a party. Clora's favorite cocktail is a margarita. Mark likes to see his wife happy. He learned how to be a better husband and father by going to church.

Shelia was making arrangements to bury Rufus. He had no insurance nor money saved. Brenda was upset because Shelia used her savings to bury Rufus. Clora brought the floral arrangement.

The wake was very nice at the funeral home. Shelia became dependent on Rufus.

He did the driving to the grocery store, her granddaughter's school, her job, the sisters' house, and other errands. Eight years of having. together, Brenda said they were living in sin. How could Shella tell people? She was a widow. Shella was married ta Willie. Clora would just listen to Brenda.

In 2008, Mark's prayer was answered. The job of his dreams comes true. The second weekend in March, his family stayed at the Sheraton Hilton. Mark's training class started Monday. He was going to Iraq and would be coming home every four months. Clora applied for a state license to open her daycare business. She would work from home. The plan was a success. Clora made sure the family attended church on Sundays. AJ graduated from Pearland High School. The Grandsons spent one weekend out of the month with the family.

Mark had brought Clora a gas grill. She invited Shelia and Brenda to her house for smoked chicken. They were amazed at the way their sister set up her business. Clora worked six-day a week. Her limit was six Children. She was licensed for twelve children. Clora brought a new SUV, furniture, clothes, and jewelry. She treated herself to the beauty salon and nail shop.

Shelia had a problem with her sister's progress. She found fault with Mark working out of the country. He left all the responsibilities to his wife. Clora learned to pray for her sister's evil spirit. Shelia never went to church service. Brenda bought an SUV. The two sisters did not like Clora supporting her husband's idea to start a business

Clora went to visit Jesse Lyn with a bag of goodies. Her niece took Jesse Lyn out of the nursing home before the first of the month. Clora was very upset and called family members for answers. She left the facility and went to the oldest niece's house. Come to find out Shelia was always in other people's mess. Brenda and Clora did not gossip with the nieces or pry into their life. The three sisters had not seen Jesse Lyn in two years. Her daughter moved to another part of town and would not let Jesse Lyn use the telephone.

Clora was busy with her life. The house Mark and his wife were leasing, the owners did not want to sell.

Mark wanted to save money and was confused about buying another house. Michelle was driving, and this was her senior year.

The three sisters were in close contact. Brenda called Clora and asked her, *"Why does Shelia hate you so much? What have you done to her?"* Shelia called Clora and asked her, *"Why is ugly Brenda jealous of you?"* Clora tried to keep peace with the sisters left. Clora would never believe her five sisters hated her. All her sisters love her.

Looking back in time, the five sisters hated that Clora knew their dark secrets. Clora was Helen's driver. Jesse Lyn's first husband tried to kill her. He was shell-shocked from the army. Helen got a phone call from the husband's aunt. Clora was on the scene being the driver. The meeting took place in the aunt's living room with Helen. Jesse Lyn was Just sitting there.

Helen and the aunt were making choices for her life. What they believe was best for Jesse Lyn or them. The plan was set in motion. The aunt made the phone call.

The family was told Jesse Lyn divorced her husband because he tried to kill her. Helen would sweep secrets under the rug. Jesse Lyn had to keep quiet. She needed therapy. Helen called her driver for Diana. Some secrets Clora found disturbing. Diana always told lies to a little girl. When Helen got to Diana's house, she was high on drugs and crying. They went into the room and talked. On the drive back to Helen s house, Diana's secret was revealed to Clora. The second secret Helen swept under the rug. Whether the incident was true or not, Diana had to move on in life.

Brenda became very good at blocking out certain events in her life. Clora drove Helen to the hospital to see Brenda. Helen loaned Brenda some money to make her secret go away. Brenda went untreated. Helen's rug was full of secrets. Brenda said Clora remembered things people wanted to forget.

Shelia was at Helen's house. Clora was told to come by the house. Helen gave Clora the instructions. She would wait at the house. Shelia and Clora were in the car talking. This was not her decision completely. Clora dropped Shelia off and picked her up a few hours later. Clora gave the bag to the lady. Shelia came out, and they got in the car. The sisters went back to Helen's house. Once Helen got the report, she swept it under the rug. Shelia was supposed to have therapy. Shelia said Clora had a brain like an elephant. She remembered everything.

Renita was the last sister living at home. She dropped out of school at sixteen years old. Every day, Renita was at Clora's apartment. She did not like being at Helen's house. Renita's secret Helen swept under the rug. She helped Renita move out of the house with Shelia. Helen did not get help for her daughters, and they could not talk about what happened. Clora knew Helen had secrets. Helen told Clora at the kitchen table. She had five weak daughters and one strong daughter.

The difference with Clora, as much as she loved her mother, she made choices for herself. The five sisters were just like Helen, believed in burying their secrets with them. Clora tried to talk about what happened. The sisters wanted the secrets to staying under the rug. Clora moved out of the big house and found a smaller place for the family.

Michelle was going to college for vocational nursing. AJ was a commission officer. Tony was close to his son. He wanted to enroll in school.

Junior was in prison for seven years. Last two years, he was working and living with his son's mother. They had a beautiful baby girl five days ago. Clora sees him every other day. His judgment and personality were unique.

Clora loves all her children equally. One child may require more attention. Each child is always able to discuss or ask questions about any topic. Mark, Clora, and her two children lived in a small town. Her husband was in Iraq. Shelia and Brenda were proud of Clora's new place.

Shelia needed to find a place to live. Her son was preparing to leave the house . Brenda was nervous about her impending retirement.

Clora was content and looking forward to spending her golden years with Mark. He was and always would be her hero. Mary, Brenda, and Shelia were discussing, had the family's old photographs. Brenda requested the photos from her niece. Mary had offended Shelia by selling the family's home. Clora was taken aback by the news. The sisters' memories of their childhood must be a combination of emotions.

Clora felt joy in her heart. Her sisters did have some happy memories. Brenda called Clora on the phone. Her job was having a workshop in Galveston. She wanted Clora to take the trip. Clora knew Brenda was scared to drive tall bridges overlooking the water. She told her sister yes.

Shelia was planning Clora's birthday celebrations for October. The three sisters were convinced that the oldest sister was also thinking of them. The four sisters had planned to get together soon. Clora, on the other hand, was equally splitting her time and love between each sister. They remained sisters to the very end.

The End

About the Author
- Clora Miller -

Clora Miller lives in Manvel, Texas. She is married to her husband of thirty-nine years and has three sons and one daughter. She attended the University of Houston for criminal justice.

This is her first book. Her goal is to write a second book and reveal the secrets and the effect each secret had on everyday life. The third book will tell how the secrets poisoned the next generation. There is help; there are resources and hotlines to help families. No one needs to live in fear or be ashamed, no matter what the secret is.

...